Building TheBrand U

5

AWESO
ME
WAYS
TO
INCREA
SE
DEPTH
INTO
YOUR
PERSO
NALITY

Dr. Anupama Mudigonda

U in the Universe Series

BUILDING THE BRAND U

5 Awesome Ways

TO

Bring Depth Into Your

Personality

Dr.Anupama Mudigonda

Mail: anupama.mudigonda@gmail.com

Dedication

To the Lotus feet of my beloved
Bhagawan, and His reflection on
earth: My Mother

Table of Contents

Building The Brand U

5 Awesome Ways to Increase Depth into Your Personality

Why is sporting a powerful self image most important in the current day scenario? Be it personal or professional life, everyone seeks a balanced and stable personality. In this overly competitive, cut-throat and fast paced world, what still remains unchanged is the credibility that is attached to a person, who is steadfast and holds integrity. "Building a Better U - 5 Awesome Ways to bring Depth into Your Personality" is a book that talks about self-image building and enhancing one's image for a better and long lasting impact. The book focuses on permanent transformations and how they can be brought about by simple, effective and actionable techniques.Building a Better U- 5 Awesome Ways to bring Depth into Your Personality compels you to revisit one's own personality and environment in the new light of delving deeper into one's own self to build a stable and balanced you. It enables you to project a powerful self- image by taking you through real case scenarios, and a set of action plans coupled with techniques that are actionable.

Read and Explore how to:

• Identify subtle behaviors and their manifestations that let others perceive you in certain ways, and learn to enhance and curb them accordingly.

• Forge long lasting and impactful relationships by self-image development.

• Avoid getting into the trap of flippancy and unfair competition.

• Expand your personality to greater depths and stop feigning what you are not.

• Avoid being shallow, and win self and others genuinely.

Preface

This is an endeavor to understand the untold, and see the less obvious. It is a conscious pursuit to hear the untold facts of life, and play our part to build a better existence for ourselves, and the others and is a part of what I call the 'U in the Universe' movement. 'U in the Universe' is a movement where I strive to make people realize that they are a part of a macrocosm, and their responsibilities stretch beyond the self to the entirety of existence as such. As a part of this series, I am coming out with these easy, operational and practical guides to equip us to contribute to the larger good. The universe is a part of us, and we a part of the universe. The universe provides for us, but the moot point is, are we reciprocating? Leave paying back in kind for the benevolence that it has ushered on us, are we even thankful to the wealth of wisdom that is inherent in us and is waiting to be unfolded? I request all the readers to understand the purpose behind the endeavor and support me in sharing these wonderful facts of life, and move towards better and evolved existence. The book is the essence of my experiences spanning over two decades and have no validation scientifically sometimes. Nevertheless, I assure you that till date no individual ever failed in these, after being mentored by me, and the testimonials of a few of my mentees shall speak for the authenticity of my school of thought.

INTRODUCTION

- How could I make people trust me?
- How can I convince my family and friends about my credibility?
- How can I let my colleagues feel that I am not shallow?
- How do I let people around me feel that they can be confident about me?

These are the questions that plague many. And many times, people feel that they are failing in winning over the confidence of significant others in their lives as well as those who matter to them. What is personality? I am not giving any psychology-based definition to this. As I keep reiterating that the techniques I share are, no doubt about human beings and their behavior, however I never go for scientific validation. For me what I understood through my own experience and observation and practice are more reliable than the written word. In my opinion personality is a unique address to an individual that distinguishes him /her from the others. It serves two major purposes:

1. It creates a unique identity to the person concerned and

2. It distinguishes him/her from the others. The personality of a person is the overall essence of a person's thoughts, behavior, actions as well as his appearance and demeanor coupled with his/her presence.

Often I feel that it's a mixed manifestation of all the physical, emotional and psychological and sometimes even meta-physical aspects of a person. It is both expressed as well as implicit. However, the impact of a personality is understood according to me in terms of how deep or shallow it tends to be.

Depth in a person is the ability of a person

to ingrain all the stimuli and exhibit his/her evolution in an even and balanced way, thereby becoming the product of experiences, learning and most importantly unlearning along with conditioning. The depth in a person always is about the concept of life, and fathoming its myriad dimensions in an even tone.

 A shallow person on the contrary, is one who is fickle and ill balanced and wavers from one stance to the other, and ends up failing ultimately. Many tell me that most of these so-called shallow personalities actually are successful. They cite several individuals-be it family members, colleagues or friends and try to explain how they lead extremely successful lives. This is true to an extent as shallowness might bring success, but it never ushers in long-term happiness. Being successful is always not synonymous with being happy. Also, life is much more beyond being materially successful. Money, power and position are definitely much required for a good life.

However, what is mandatory for peace and success is lasting happiness and balanced life that is possible only when an individual evolves internally and experiences inner depth and tranquility.

Having said that, I have observed that deep personalities are always not positive. So, in this book I have limited myself to positive aspects of depth and only refer to how positive depth can be carefully nurtured into our personalities to enrich our lives with hope and progress.

Why do we want depth in our personality? Well, each one of us evolves and we want to progress, and also manifest the development in terms of being better in our thoughts, actions, expressions and behavior. Each one us wants to belong and extend herself/himself through the relationships one has in life. Every individual aspires to be that part of his family, society and community that comes across as balanced and praise worthy. To top it all, we want to be cherished and would love to be a part of like-minded associations and strive to be of some importance to self and others.

This book is an endeavor to throw some light on small things that make a lot of difference in shaping your personality, as well as the way these contribute to the perception of others of you. In order to make this complicated issue simple and actionable, I have listed out five ways to bring depth to an individual, and help build a credible image that I would discuss in detail about. They are:

1. Treat every person and thing with respect.
2. Think for others
3. Don't be flippant
4. Be balanced
5. Just BE don't feign

Chapter 1
Treat every person and thing with respect...

Well, there is a reason for everything, and it goes without saying that credibility is something that can be earned only by being meticulously working on one's own self. Apart from the inborn nature of a person, it needs to be built consciously by reflecting on every action that one takes, and every experience that one undergoes.

Positive Behaviour & Personality Reflecors

	Behaviour	PERCEIVED PERSONALITY TRAITS	
	Taking care of stuff, handing over and safekeeping for self. and even others:	• Responsible. • Trustworthy and • Loving	
	Not accepting responsibilities when one cannot deliver and not bowing down to cajoling and emotional blackmail:	• Credibility and integrity • Strength of will and • Strength of character.	
	Sharing food, chores or work along with other activities and responsibilities:	• Friendly nature, • Warm personality and • Loving and kind disposition.	
	Neately kept stuff and esthetically arranged rooms, tables and living/work spaces:	• Meticulous, • Energetic and • Vibrant personality.	
	Responsive behavior with immediate feedback and communication	• Affable and lovable • High concern for others	
	Stable disposition and balanced lifestyle with little fluctuations in reactions and general behavior:	• Reliable and • Sensible.	
	Giving importance to others time and money as well as efforts:	• Empathetic and • Loving nature.	
	Standing by and helping and filling up others with hope and positivity along with self:	• Success/goal-oriented • Blanced personality	
	Responding to requests and communicating clearly and expressing feelings and thoughts clearly and pleasantly	• Genuine personality • Credibility.	
	Extending self to be inclusive and accommodate others with in means and allowing for others to be themselves accepting them as they are	• Wholesomeness and • Wonderful disposition.	

The first way to bring depth into oneself is to treat every person and thing with respect.

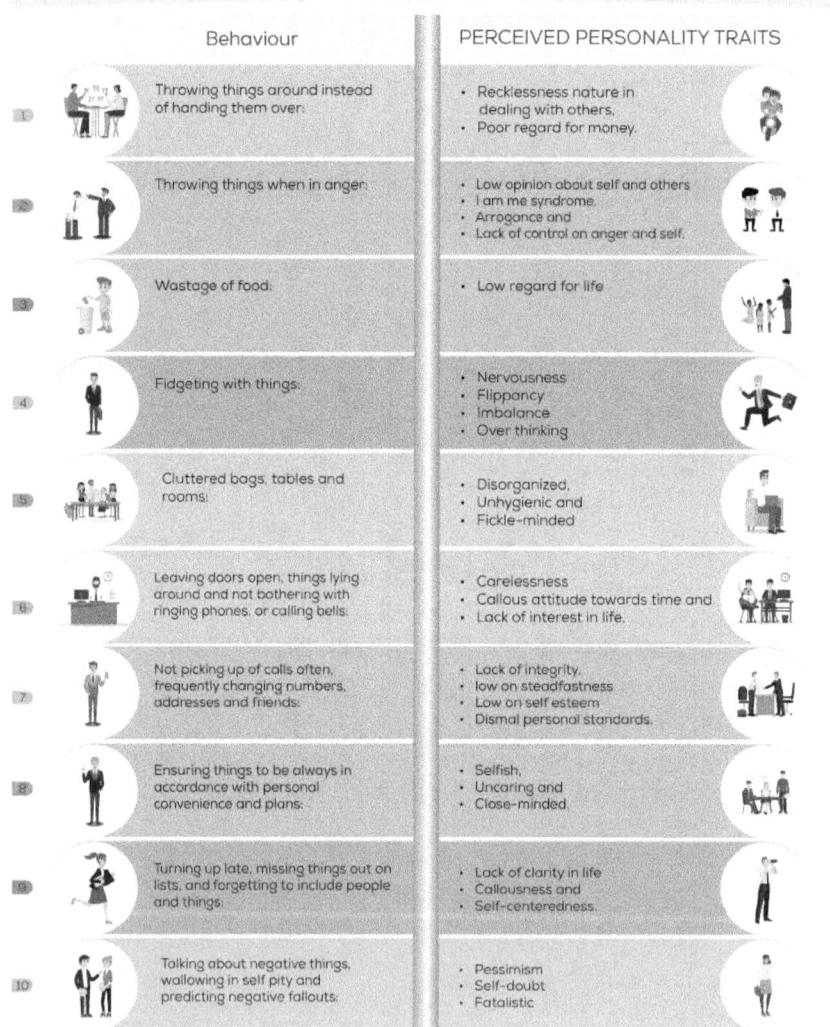

UNWANTED (NEGATIVE) BEHAVIOUR AND ITS REFLECTIONS ON ONES PERSONALITY

	Behaviour	PERCEIVED PERSONALITY TRAITS	
1	Throwing things around instead of handing them over:	• Recklessness nature in dealing with others, • Poor regard for money.	
2	Throwing things when in anger:	• Low opinion about self and others • I am me syndrome. • Arrogance and • Lack of control on anger and self.	
3	Wastage of food:	• Low regard for life	
4	Fidgeting with things:	• Nervousness • Flippancy • Imbalance • Over thinking	
5	Cluttered bags, tables and rooms:	• Disorganized, • Unhygienic and • Fickle-minded	
6	Leaving doors open, things lying around and not bothering with ringing phones, or calling bells:	• Carelessness • Callous attitude towards time and • Lack of interest in life.	
7	Not picking up of calls often, frequently changing numbers, addresses and friends:	• Lack of integrity, • low on steadfastness • Low on self esteem • Dismal personal standards.	
8	Ensuring things to be always in accordance with personal convenience and plans:	• Selfish, • Uncaring and • Close-minded.	
9	Turning up late, missing things out on lists, and forgetting to include people and things:	• Lack of clarity in life • Callousness and • Self-centeredness.	
10	Talking about negative things, wallowing in self pity and predicting negative fallouts:	• Pessimism • Self-doubt • Fatalistic	

Things to be treated with respect? *What's that?* Many of you may wonder. Trust me; it does make a difference as to how you treat yourself, people around you, and even inanimate things around you. The way we go about taking care of things around us also makes a statement about our personality. For example, dust lying everywhere in your living room, would tell people what kind of a person you are. More so, ill-kept lawns, shabbily kept cup-boards and cluttered tables, and living places scream out to the others that you are not organized and you don't bother about cleanliness. From your office desk to your kitchen counter, worse still, the way you stack your refrigerator, or how you handle an electronic appliance, gives insights into your personality to the world. Also many people have a callous attitude towards inanimate things. They toss them over while handing them to others, and don't bother to properly maintain, run and dispose them, when they no longer serve their need. This does make others jittery about dealing with such people, as our habits might give subconscious signals about our inner self to others. **Respect people for what they are: The tiny tip** a small boy entered a roadside restaurant and the waiter appraised his appearance and found that he was grubby and looked hungry. Thinking that he was there to ask for some extra food, the waiter told him off saying that left over food can be had

Only between ten and eleven in the night after the restaurant closed. The boy smiled and said he had enough money to pay for his food and that he came to eat an ice cream, which he always wanted to but couldn't ever. He was promptly seated. The waiter found that the boy struggled with the menu and tried to help him by asking which flavor he wanted to eat. The boy searched and asked for his dream choice and its price.

The waiter said it would cost him seventy-five rupees. The boy checked his purse and asked for another flavor and was told that it cost him seventy rupees.

The boy went for the later. The waiter became busy with other tables after serving the boy and the boy left after paying his bill. As the waiter went to clean his table on the plate he found a five-rupee tip. I heard this somewhere, and thought as to how beautiful was the boy's way of expressing his respect for those who served him. He cut down on his personal agenda to honor someone who served him. People around us sub consciously send signals that can be interpreted to reveal their inner traits and their nature. Many things that we do subconsciously, flash signals that scream about what we are all about. Many times we see people and assume their traits gauging the way they speak to senior citizens or the way they think of their country. These are not foolproof mechanisms, and might be wrong too but by nurturing our personality with positivity we might not fall into this trap. How can one detect these and avoid them is the next pertinent question. Well, like always I would only suggest that whatever we do, it must be genuine and should be done after accepting it with all our heart. If you follow any of the self-help techniques without understanding their significance and expanse, I am sure you will end up half-baked and phony. So before we even discuss these traits let me once again warn you that any techniques or insights related to the self and self-concept need to be understood from an individual perspective, and should be followed and practiced with utmost sincerity for the best results thereof. It is impossible to list out all the different manifestations of behaviors and relate them to possible traits in personality. May I remind you again that the list given is just the tip of an iceberg, and there could be much more to this? However, I made a list ten of the possible connotations of some of these behaviors -both positive, and negative for understanding this concept better.

Positive Behavior and Personality Reflectors:

The behavioral manifestations of inherent positive attributes to one's personality and the traits there of are listed as below:

Negative Behavior and Personality Reflectors

The unwanted behavioral manifestations connote certain negative traits in an individual and here is a list of few such reflectors: So, having gone through the positive and negative hints that our behavior subconsciously sends to people, we need to carefully and meticulously ingrain certain personal standards to allow for evolution with in. Any kind of artificial put on behavior would only make things worse. That is because, if we just showcase behavior that we actually don't prescribe to in reality, it goes without saying that we live a life of pretense and it by no means would make us happy in any way. It might gain short-term victories, but in the long run it would prove to be a personal disaster. How to learn to respect people and things? People often ask me this question, as they say mostly they find individuals acting so out of depth that they just can't come round to give them any kind of respect. And regarding things, many opine that inanimate things must be treated so, and there shouldn't be any attachment to material things. Their logic being, after all, they can always be replaced.

Here is a set of ten action plans for you to develop respect for others—animate or inanimate:

1. *Respect yourself:* If you respect yourself, then automatically you would respect others too, as if you respect others and self, then you gain their respect in return.

2. *Respect others for what they stand for:* Respect individuals for their values, work or patience. Life must be celebrated and what better way it could be than to celebrate people for all the wonderful ways in which they influence the world.

3. *Respect people for what they aren't:* Did we ever take a minute and try to respect people for what they aren't? We are full of criticism for those who are selfish or exhibit bad behavior, but did we ever acknowledge or appreciate those who are balanced and pleasant to be with? Do we ever appreciate people for not being selfish, fickle or imbalanced? It's time we do that by showing respect to such wonderful human beings.

4. *Respect things:* If you don't treat gadgets with respect, they would work

for lesser time, than stimulated and you would be penalized for that. Also, a gadget or thing needs to be handled the way it should be, for longer and better experiences of usage. Respect here can be proper maintenance, timely refills and repairs and keeping the gadgets, gismos and tools well oiled, covered and cleaned regularly.

5. *Respect others thoughts and feelings:* Listen to others sincerely. Mostly, people get to know how much you respect them when you give them a patient ear. Listening to what people have to say and understanding between the lines is the best way of respecting anyone.

6. *Respect the strengths but do acknowledge the flaws:* One must always be loved for both one's strengths and high points and as well as one's flaws. More so on flaws as we

all love the lovable aspects of a personality but the depth in us grows, as we understand that even the flaws are a part of one's personality and make way for that. You would naturally be respecting them for what they are, rather than having a prejudiced view of their personality.

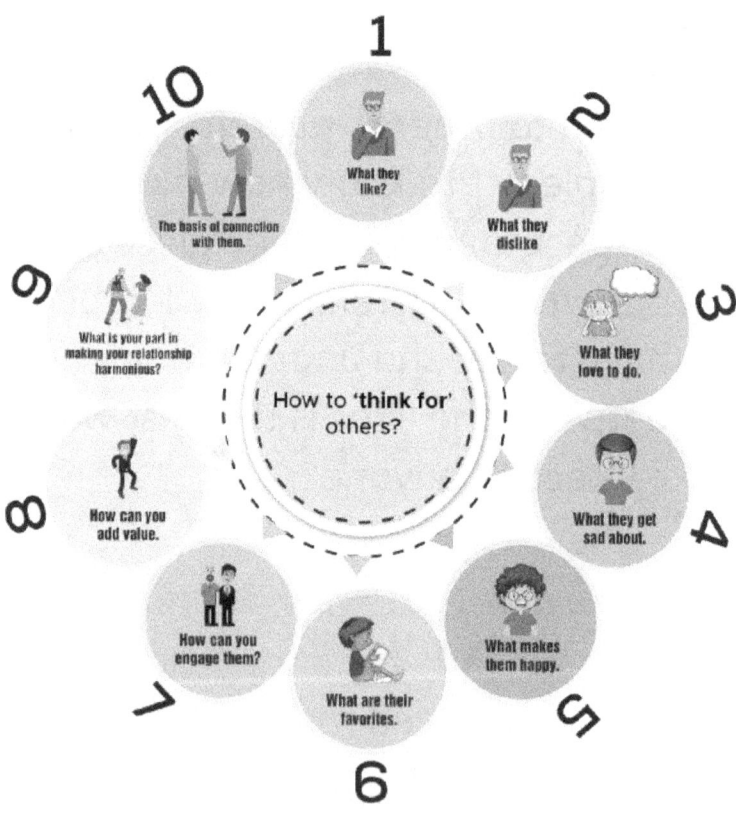

7. *Respect others opinions:* Be respectful towards others' opinions, even though you don't subscribe to them. Remember, as you have yours, they have their own way of looking at life and living it. After all everyone has a right to her/his opinion.

8. *Maintain self and others dignity at all costs:* If you don't take on others' dignity, they usually never encroach on yours. So never trespass on others' dignity. This is the best way to bring loads of depth as people respect those who respect their boundaries.

9. *Be tolerant to others*: Tolerance it is the first and ground rule of being human. Hence it is but natural for us to accept diversity in thought, habits culture, faith or intellect and ideology. If we appreciate the beauty in diversity, our personality deepens to accommodate for new and better

insights into self. Lack of aggression breeds amicability, thereby winning us the trust and acknowledgement from others who feel safe with us.

These ten action plans are just the beginning, and I am sure that as we fathom ourselves, we learn that there is always more to dwell on to develop. Progressive thinking and being are two most important tenets of expanding our personality, and they grow manifold when we develop a sense of respect for all-the inanimate and animate.

Chapter 2
Think For Others

Often I get emails, greeting cards and text messages that say, "Thinking of you!" So far so good, but I feel most elated when someone chips in saying, "I had been thinking for you, and I feel you would love to listen to this piece of music, or you might like to go through this article." Well, thinking of others no doubt gives a sense of wellbeing amongst all of us and connects us with our friends, colleagues and family. However, depth comes into relationships when we think for people. But, how is 'thinking of' different from 'thinking for'? I realized that 'thinking of' is passive mostly, while 'thinking for' is active and action oriented. When we think of people, it is usually because we miss them. We miss our family, friends and partners and thinking of them is but natural. However, 'thinking of' although is spontaneous, it is very shallow, as it often turns into obsession with unproductive after effects.

We think for people when we want to contribute to their success, well-being or simply their happiness. This immediately would transform into a gesture and that

would bring around over all joy, both for the giver, as well as the receiver of the experience. In short, thinking of could be pining away and is unproductive and often infectious. However, Thinking for could be a very realistic practical and better way of communicating our affection for people we love. I selected five instances just for an understanding of what I was trying to explain. Here is a simple comparison of, 'Thinking of' and 'Thinking for' ...

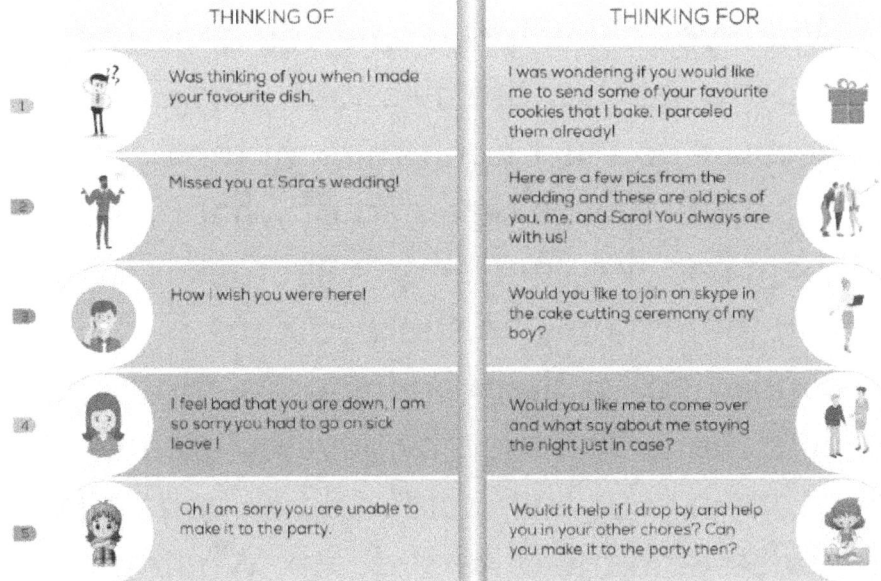

THINKING OF	THINKING FOR
Was thinking of you when I made your favourite dish.	I was wondering if you would like me to send some of your favourite cookies that I bake. I parceled them already!
Missed you at Sara's wedding!	Here are a few pics from the wedding and these are old pics of you, me, and Sara! You always are with us!
How I wish you were here!	Would you like to join on skype in the cake cutting ceremony of my boy?
I feel bad that you are down. I am so sorry you had to go on sick leave!	Would you like me to come over and what say about me staying the night just in case?
Oh I am sorry you are unable to make it to the party.	Would it help if I drop by and help you in your other chores? Can you make it to the party then?

Thinking for people is a more responsible and

wholesome exercise when compared to thinking of people. It is a very good way of cultivating depth into our personality by allowing our faculties to think for others and try to be of some productive value to people other than self. I listed out a few of the pre-requisites for developing this habit of thinking for people. These are not fool proof, yet they cover most of the basic aspects of connecting with others while spreading affection for them, and thereby rendering our own personality deeper. When you think for people you need to know what they are all about. This is because you just don't think of them, but you are trying to be a part of what makes them happy or better or what makes you and them happy. In short you are concerned for them and your relationship with them. You thereby develop greater depth in your own personality when you understand the others' depth. What makes them inspired, happy or sad, what ticks people off. Imagine knowing these small details and acting accordingly so that every meeting you have with them is full of mutual love and r e s p e c t a n d spontaneously so, as although you learnt about them, your reactions and genuineness would set them to reciprocate and strengthen the bonding. Over a period of time you would develop spontaneity in these issues too.

The Action Plan. I would like to propose my own indigenous theory, which I call as the **Every Encounter Positive Encounter (EEPE)** technique, which most of my followers say is a very effective technique in dealing with others and enriching relationships. ***Every***

Encounter Positive Encounter (EEPE): I suggested this initially for important or significant others in our lives. However later on many said that they extended it to even absolute strangers and found it be super effective. And why not! The technique is very simple and is a win-win tool.

EEPE as the name suggests prescribes a hassle-free interaction and engagement tone when we interact with others. Most of the time I find people to be opinionated and very fickle on one hand about their realities and their way of looking at life and others, while on the other side, there are always those bunch of not-so-sure individuals who are forever hanging around unsure of what they are at. Well this is a good remedy for everyone who aims to weave his/her way softly through the jungle of complex human beings.

EEPE is based on the theory that no matter what, there is something good about every person. However bad he or she may be, it cannot be that they are not good at something. For a positive interaction, a single positive point is enough to build a huge positive experience on it. It is very easy to nag at others, or point out their flaws, but it takes a lot to detect the inner worth, and that aspect t of the individual, which i s commendable e no matter what. By concentrating on finding out the positive aspects of a person, we are deviating from fault-finding to a more productive proactive trait-finding exercise, which would not only reduce negativity within us towards the others, but also earn us extra points for detecting and endorsing others' worth,

There by putting us in good stead as far as they are concerned. Often I found nasty people to be good in organizing things, and found a few to have great acumen in dealing with difficult people. An individual can be snubbed for his short-tempered nature, however you have a pleasant surprise from him/ her if you notice and encourage him in some other thing he is good at. Basically the entire exercise is to look at good things and respect people for it, rather than count on their flaws and make them miserable. Please try the tool, which has the following three steps in it.

1. Meet and deal with people on a positive note. This includes:

- Genuine warmth in greeting b. speaking pleasantly and with a smile
- Discussing and remembering fondly, good experiences/ memories that are shared by both parties.
- Wishing well for each other, and
- Being unobtrusive about personal spaces and prejudices.

2. Turn a simple, negative or hostile, in fact every kind of meet up into a positive one:

- Always tell people what you admire about them (genuinely).
- Always bank on the positive points and strengths and avoid the negative points. Discuss any

unpleasantness on a positive note like, "It's unfortunate that this had to happen but I think it can be easily sorted out if we can get together on it."

- Make room for others' insights and opinions and ideas.

3. Part on a super positive note:

- Express your joy over meeting the person, and thank for any hospitality extended.
- Hand over a small token of remembrance that sets a pace for a wonderful reunion.
- Say goodbye by acknowledging how much the time spent with them meant to you.
- Drop a message immediately after the meeting, reiterating the point that you enjoyed their company.

Chapter 3
Don't be Flippant

Oh he is such a show off!!" A woman

whispered into my ears looking at a
gentleman who was trying to entertain

everyone at the get together. "But he is only trying to make it lively!" I

defended the stranger out of habit. I just can't stand anyone being talked ill about.

"Oh c'mon! What do you know about him! " The woman was on fire.

"He tries to make everyone else feel very insignificant. He barges in on conversations, and rubbishes people's claims and he always wants to be in the limelight. See? It's his friend's day today, and you know what is happening. And the best part is, he thinks he is smart!" My friend grumbled rolling her eyes.

What is flippancy? A very despicable attitude of disrespect towards others. This could be both overt, and/or subtle. Many a time I wonder if people even know they are exhibiting such an attitude. I usually find at least a couple of such people everywhere I go. It goes without saying that, this also can take the form of passive aggression if it's not thwarted in the initial stages. These individuals try to 'steal the show' and want to let others know that they are the center of attraction. However, while many tell me this is dominance due to self-aggrandizement or thinking too highly of self, I beg to differ here, as I find people who are so to be lacking in self-esteem resorting to such means. That is actually the opposite of what many people believe in. Those who are sought after and popular never need to steal the show. While those who are in eternal self-doubt want to prove to the world that they are the best.

There are many reasons why people tend to be flippant. However experiences in life, brought up, attitudinal anomalies and fear of losing one's position in the family due to insecurity, society or at work, are some of the reasons according to me that make people resort to flippancy. A few kinds of behavior's I noticed in such people are:

- Omitting people who they feel are a threat to them.

- Sabotage or resort to non-cooperation with a possible 'rival'
- Crashing on a conversation and trying to dominate it.
- Weaning the topic towards self, and trying to quote self-experiences whether relevant or not
- Feeding gossip and allowing people to think I'll of others by goading on controversial topics about the individual or situation.

T : Is it true?
H : Is it helpful?
I : Is it Inspiring?
N : Is it necessary?
K : Is it kind?

These are only a few, however in reality, flippancy has no limit, nor any scruples. But the mute point is, how does one get over this? Well, the best panacea for this would be to make room for others genuinely. Or better still try behaving and being someone who is really a show-stealer that is being a hearty and a splendid person in earnest. The easiest way is to let others be and thrive on inclusion of others rather than their omission.

Techniques to effectively overcome flippancy:

Some of the techniques that I found very effective in overcoming this attitude are:

1. *Deliberately allowing others a chance to express.* For example one can allow others to

The situation/ person or issue checklist	Your observation
Are you saying the Truth/ did you hear the truth?	
Is it going to **Help** you or others if you express?	
Would you **Inspire** others by saying what you are planning to?	
Is it **Necessary** to talk about it?	
Are you being **Kind**/unkind to someone if you say/do whatever you have planned to?	

Speak without interruption every second time in a conversation. It's not so difficult once you make a habit of letting others express and finish their talk, and then speak.

A. Stop being manipulative and let the

stuff unfold naturally, and look for yourself how you fare. If your personality shows through that's a fantastic outcome. If not, you know you avoided being flippant. So a win-win for you.

B. Genuinely endorsing others for whatever it is worth. For example, if you are popular for singing, you may want to introduce a fellow colleague, friend or family member, who is a good instrumentalist, saying that she/he entertains better, and also do a duet with the person just to encourage them.

C. Letting others thrive along with you. We can always show case our talent, while allowing others to showcase theirs too.

D. Set the tone by endorsing others, and they would reciprocate. It is but natural for people to feel good and humbled when we endorse them for their expertise or personality. If you endorse others instead of trying to overrule them to get popular, they would definitely return compliments by endorsing you. Even if they don't, you still would be thought of as an affable individual who supports others.

How do we refrain from being flippant? Well I am sharing a few tips here:

An instant Activity for curbing flippancy It is difficult to practice these but it is never impossible. An easier way I figured out to curb impulsive behavior is to follow the acronym THINK before we act.

T: Is it true?
H: Is it helpful?
I: Is it Inspiring?
N: Is it necessary?
K: Is it kind?

The acronym and the related questions are a quick checklist that we must go through before we speak or do anything. This might bring down careless talk on our behalf and improve our personal worth by making us less flippant.

The 'Check your Flippancy' table:
Evaluate yourself and this exercise would first of all slow you down on doing something in an off-the cuff manner. It would also make you weigh the pros and cons of broaching something that would not be in the interest of your personal image building. Flippancy always hints at the shallowness of a person. People often

lose the edge they have in being witty, successful or knowledgeable when they are flippant. It is to be understood that none likes those who try to flaunt themselves. One may be popular in the short run by being flippant, but I am sure none of us likes people who are full of themselves, and are disrespectful towards others. Dig deeper into your personality, and find reasons for trusting others and giving them space, as well as their due. Nurturing the environment we are in as important as self-growth. When we try to manipulate and overpower people around us, we tend to focus our energies away from self-expansion and that immediately renders us shallow. It is a win-win strategy to allow the natural progression of our personality and the recognition and spread thereof, rather than forcefully trying to outshine people around us.

Chapter 4

Be Balanced

The fourth important dimension to develop depth in ourselves is to be balanced. All of us know that it is easier said than done. Most of us know and have seen how difficult it is to be balanced in all the situations and at all times. It is tough but isn't impossible though. If you want to consciously be balanced, then it would be a tall order. However, if you cultivate balance in your very being, I feel after all its not going to be not so difficult. This brings us to the question what is being balanced? For some it is staying indifferent and for others it is being presentable. Technically being balanced means being in a position of equilibrium. This in turn means a person who acts the same in the highs and lows of life. However, practically and realistically speaking, a perfect state of balance is impossible to be maintained. Moreover human dynamics call for a different definition of being balanced and this would change every time the situation and the context changes. If you ask me, I would always say that a balanced person is the one who thinks acts and expresses in a way that is relatively fair and even.

Now, what do I mean by that? We'll let us list out a balanced person's characteristics according to what I could garner in about two decades.

Traits of a balanced person:
A person who is balanced:
1. Is progressive

2. Is not abrupt

3. Tends to weigh the pros and cons and takes a fair decision in a given situation.

4. Believes in freedom of thought and expression of everyone.

5. Is objective basing the choice on facts?

6. Has the inner strength to take adversities and accolades in stride.

7. Knows how to communicate.

8. Is perfect in timing communication.

9. Bases the decision making on past experiences and logic.

10.   Considers the implications of actions before tackling any issue.

How do we achieve this seemingly impossible state of mind? I can list out a few techniques that may help you practice this very tough state of existence and I assure you, repeated and continuous adherence to these techniques would usher in a semblance of balance in any individual.

1. Develop clarity about:

      A. Self Who you are/ are not What you want Who you want to be with How you wish to live your life

      B. Situation who is involved What are the dynamics How to address, tackle or overcome

      C. Others what they stand for what motivates or aggravates them How to reach out to them/ tackle them

2.   Be objective:

A very tough but, a very possible

habit. Never bring bias into your outlook, as it ruins self. The moment we base our plans thoughts and actions on bias, we lose already. Facts, figures and reality-based thoughts and decisions are more practical than assumptions, prejudices and hunches.

The easiest way to stay objective is to differentiate our bases for thinking into two absolutely separate compartments based on their sources. Those that have a source in us and those that comes from a reputed or trusted outside source. By saying this I by no means am belittling our innate sense of judgment and intuition. However, I would like to warn against egotism and self-aggrandizement against honest and unbiased evaluation of facts. Some of the usual clashes that occur in this regard can be because of individuals thinking from their view point rather that what the world believes in. very simply said, it is a comparison between what 'I like' versus' what 'it should be'. Individual belief system vs. the general and commonly accepted belief system is the cause for most of the imbalances, and it is an offshoot of continuous evolution that happens, as mankind evolves

3. **Believe in the 50-50 theory always:** Having said that one must be active; it might seem that I am paradoxical when I say believe in a 50-50 theory. I developed this theory very early in life, like in my high school, as I found out that no matter what, it's only from your side that you know of something and can plan and execute something.

The rest of the fifty percent of the same remains with the universe and is open to its dynamics. In short don't ever assume that you are in total control of everything. Always remember that anything could happen that might be contrary to our understanding of the situation. So it is important we school our mind to be ready for any kind of deviation or eventuality to stay balanced.

4. Practice silence-external and internal

This very fetching technique as silence when embraced in its essence breeds thought and depth. Silence used as a mode of passive aggression, or for combat purposes however, would not yield any productive results other than delaying an immediate confrontation. What is external silence? Simply put, it is reducing the number of words spoken and even the decibel levels. That is talking less. Allowing for less noise around us as in use of gadgets, avoiding clichés and being overtly expressive about anything and everything are also means of reducing noise in a different level. And I would like to clarify here that talking less doesn't mean becoming an emotional recluse by being non-expressive. I only recommend for clarity in thought to express things in few words and intersperse it with silence. In the current age of information explosion and noise pollution, I feel that the individual space is contaminated with harsh noises that jar our thinking and feeling quotients. I often find that constant noises that include our own generated noises ruin our faculties and render them blunt and rust them as we have become so overt these days giving so much of importance to expression and articulation, that we have lost the ability to see the beauty of subtlety. For example, loud music and so-called 'output oriented music' has relegated the melody aspect to the background. Noise in every form rules us, while our sense go blunt as every stimulus is overpowering and hits us deliberately invoking a reaction. In this context, the natural phenomenon of listening to, soaking in and interpreting the stimulus is lost somewhere. These days every stimulus is in anticipation of a reaction I feel. There is no room for any kind of inner understanding and absorption in this kind of a scenario. So I suggest that one must practice external silence. When we practice external silence we tend to exhibit a sort of decorum that compels the others to respect and follow suit. It creates a platform for a dialogue instead of confrontation and it also becomes the foreground for a stable and clutter-free thought and action process. External silence is more of the physical aspect, while internal silence deals with metaphysics and psychological state of mind. When silence is practiced internally, it paves the way for the fertility of mind. Thoughts and emotions that emanate from a calm interior always are rich in clarity and are well balanced. Internal silence can be best achieved by following simple meditation techniques. How do we practice external silence and cultivate internal silence? Well, here are a few tips for the same:

External Silence

- Talk less and express more

- Surround yourself with silence as much as possible

- Avoid loud and shrill noises like ring tones and calling bells/ alarms •Speak in a low soothing voice.

- Avoid shouting at all times.

- Talk only when necessary

Internal silence

- Don't clutter your mind with

unnecessary information

- Fill your mind with purpose of life-temporary, as well as long-term

- Think only to the extent possible. Leave the rest to the universe
- Avoid manipulations and negativity
- Never lose focus

Being silent always brings a certain depth to our personality, as silence is often infectious. It tends to make the people around feel calm and serene when productive, confused and subdued when passive, and threatened and agitated when aggressive. It is for us to decide as to how we want to use this beautiful gift- as a weapon, as a shield or as a tool to craft harmony and balance for self and others.

5. Stall reactions The true test of being balanced as they say is not to jump your guns. Acting on impulse is the exact opposite to reacting to stimuli without a thought. The best way to stay balanced is to take your time to react. This would always arrest any kind of immediate precipitation and unnecessary escalation of unwanted reactions from your end. Also, it paves the way for a more even and tempered response that would no doubt be a better option than immediate outburst.

6. **Give importance to timing** One of the most important and oft not followed techniques of staying balanced is practicing the sense of timing. Many a time, a well-meant communication or action might be misinterpreted and misunderstood because of wrong timing. It is very important for an individual to cultivate the discipline to wait for the right time to act or express. Well-timed interventions not only save us embarrassments, but also multiply the impact of the same manifold without any extra effort form our side.

7. Avoid a sense of finality A more rational approach to being balanced is to understand the fact that nothing is permanent. Many time we often find dramatic expressions by individuals who tend to be foreboding by saying that a particular decision or act or words spoken were final. Well, I think and for sure know that death is the only finality in life. Other than that I strongly feel that one must avoid this gesture, as nothing is predictable about human dynamics and the interplay of emotions, situations and people. I sincerely would suggest everyone to avoid inducing this false sense of finality just to gain weight to their expression and in return losing their balance. No matter what, we must all remember that there is every chance that we might encounter a similar or the same person, situation or expression/outcome. So as long as it lasts, we tackle, bear or live with it, and then are prepared to face it even in future, by learning to deal with such eventualities rather than making ominous prophesies.

8. Abstain from being and sounding like a 'know-all': Pretense is one facet of a personality that robs one of authenticity. A balanced person never pretends as it takes away the equilibrium that emanates from knowledge and integrity. What we don't know, we don't! And the best way to tackle our ignorance is to accept it and learn by asking or seeking. Instead we find most people feigning that they know and then making fools of themselves. Asking makes us not only truthful and humble but also makes us look humane. There is no rule that one must know everything! It is wonderful to accept once ignorance and seek knowledge than hide it.

9. Allow things to be solved in their own time A stich in time says nine, they say and it is true. However sometimes we either don't know how many stiches or when should we be stitching, should we be doing it, and where do we actually mend. In that case it's better to wait and let things take a natural course rather than barging in and spoiling any chances of betterment. This is especially in case of psychological aspects of a person as well as resolving issues with self and others. It is never a great idea to intervene between two individuals. We must try to bring people together no doubt, but not at the cost of their individual space. Moreover intense psychological conditions might warrant time for the individual (s) to coup and reorient themselves to the fact of the matter.

10. Let there be empathy A perfect way to attaining balance in life is to see others in the same light as we see ourselves. Avoiding bias against individuals may be really

Action Plan
•Be realistic and don't make tall promises

•Be truthful to yourself before being to others
•Be original and never try to pretend or ape
•Be with/have clarity of thought and action
•Be focused

Difficult but if we try to reverse it and extend the bias that we reverse for ourselves and our actions to others, then I think we can develop empathy towards others easily. Al I the special considerations that we keep reserved for self, all the standards that we erect for self, if we can extend them to the others than the world would definitely a better place to live.

Chapter 5
Just Be-don't feign

The last point of my discussion is definitely the most pertinent of them all. It encompasses all the other techniques that have been discussed above. I would like to emphasize on it more than any other technique, as all the techniques discussed above would fail if one doesn't follow the rigor mentioned here. No matter what you do how you think or act, if you aren't genuine, there wouldn't be any difference to your behavior or persona. To usher more depth into your personality, you must concentrate on being genuine about what you stand up for. Many a time we come across superficial personalities who do not follow their own words.

Be it personal life or professional arena, those individuals who stand by what they say and promise what they deliver are always considered being trustworthy.

One need not be a hi-flying successful individual for this. One just needs to stick to ones guns and that is all there is to it. It is as easy as that. However practicing this is not as easy as we say, and as it appears. Constant adherence to self-set standards and following a self-defined path of behavior always is not possible given the vagaries and ups and downs of life.

However it is also a fact that man is an animal of habits, and as you feed on bad habits so would you on good habits. So one can always train self in following a well-defined practical and realistic path of what one says and delivering on them.

Action Plan to Develop Credibility:

The following are the action pointers for being a credible individual:

1. Be realistic and don't make tall promises:

How can you be consistent? Well the answer is by being realistic in your thought and approach. It's common for most of us to say when asked that when we would be able to deliver something, that we would do it that very day or next day etc. It's a small test to see how realistic we are, coz most of the time we never calculate the actual time. Most of the time we do it to diffuse tensions about deadlines and also to eliminate stress for others in the system be it family or colleagues. However in doing so for short-term results we tend to bring down our credibility. Missing on deliverables and deadlines consistently brings down our worth. When tall promises are made and are not followed up by actions, the damage done is quadrupled when compared to simple promises broken. That's the reason why we must never take up more than what we can chew. Doing things within our means and accepting challenges that are relatively within our extended prowess is much better bet than taking up on something, which we are not sure of.

2. **Be truthful to yourself before being to others:**

The issue that is often discussed these days is about a person not being in tune with self. Expressions like, 'does she even know what she is doing?' To 'he doesn't know what he is up to and who would tell him/her this?" are gaining common ground as individuals are getting removed from self-reality more and more. Individuals are losing track of what they stand for and what they are all about, as people are carried away by their ideas about self rather than facing the reality. Objective self-assessment is being rapidly replaced by you know yourself concept where people no longer heed to an honest feedback.

3. Be original and never try to pretend or ape:

A more often repeated issue that causes serious impediments in attaining deeper personality traits is pretense. Aping someone or pretending to be something that we actually are not brings down the personality.

4. Be with clarity of thought and action: A very significant ingredient in the successful development of one's personality is having clarity with regards to thoughts and actions. I observed that this is often an offshoot of having our facts and faculties in place. Those who set their priorities right often emerge better equipped to combat the challenges of life than those who are unsure of the facts and outcomes. A clear understanding of situation and a well thought of stand, based on facts and experience and wise counsel often induces clarity in thought and actions resulting in adding more depth to our personalities.

5. Be focused:

It goes without saying that having a specific goal in mind and working towards is much better than groping in uncertainty being clueless. As such most of the situations life presents us with are not under our control. However, it presents us with the very premise for being focused and be well equipped to deal with the dynamics of the situation. A concerted effort aligned with our goals and resources as well as faculties would always make us face life with confidence rather than a very shaky stance that wavers at the face every challenge. What does one need for ingraining these qualities? First and foremost one must have a habit of **acceptance of the truth about self** for what it is without finding someone or something to blame. An individual needs lots of **courage** to accept his flaws and work on them to dissipate the negative fallouts of the same. Apart from the above what one needs is a relatively **large heart** to accept and imbibe feedback, as well as learn from past experiences.

In order for an individual to develop him selves into a practical and credible person, she/he must sport a **simple and clutter free mind.**

This is very important as a mind full of doubts, confusion and ambiguity makes the person to oscillate continuously and this would take him/her from stability. A person can only match his or her words to actions, when he or she has the **attitude to accomplish things** for what they are.

A casual attitude often results in missing out on details and makes a person appear shallow, as he/ she tends to miss depth in the situation. **A high acceptance rate** of what happens with us is the next prerequisite to build a steadfast image of oneself. No matter what, accepting things makes it easy to move on and think about what next rather than mopping over the past. The sooner the acceptance, the faster and profound are the lessons learnt and the more progressive is the evolution of such individuals.

I personally feel that we need to reiterate for ourselves time and again some tenets that would always make us revisit ourselves and give us the strength to move forward without getting intimidated by the people or situations around us. I call these my personal commandments and whenever I face any kind of situation in life where my equilibrium is threatened I reiterate them and find strength.

Positive affirmations for self-confidence

•You are who you are! (Everyone is unique)
•Your abilities are yours no matter what. (Everyone has a special ability in this universe)

•Your likes and dislikes are based on your personality and experiences in life. (Every one is a byproduct of his own drama called life)

•Your subscription to any ideology is purely on the basis of your understanding and acceptance of the same. (Everyone has his Master plan)

•You have flaws and weaknesses and so do others (None is perfect)You have a right to your opinion. (To each, his own) How do we get motivated to follow this rigor? It doesn't take much actually as when you know what people like about others generally and what they despise about. We must know these in order for us to relate to the significant others and shape our social self as well as develop personally also

We must know that people don't like:

•Those who try to feign and pretend.

•Those who try to project their personality differently from what it is,

•Those who prevaricate about things just to suit themselves

•Those who never stand up for what they are

•Those who never stand by in times of need

•Those who don't have time for others

•Those who don't listen and only want to talk

•Those who are critical of anything and everything

•Those who are unsure of things all the time. It brings home the point that our personality is not just the few expressions of our inner self but it's the totality of all that we stand for. It is our nature, our attitude, our experiences in life and the impact of the same on our thoughts behavior and action thereof. So it is always the best bet to showcase what we are rather than feign what we are not. It is a fact that people do understand that one cannot be flawless, and so inherently do not mind if others are imperfect.

Conclusion

Every personality is like a book that cannot be judged by its cover. However, a thorough work on self is much warranted, as we build ourselves into credible individuals. Life is a quest for harmony and self-discovery and developing depth in one's personality is not only the by-product of it, but also the wonderful fruit of practicing what we learn from our own encounters with life. I hope that this book helps you in chalking your way through yourself. The five techniques that I discussed here are time tested, simple and practical. All you need is patience, a little bit of ingenuity and loads of forethought. The action plans discussed in the book are all realistic and action worthy. The techniques I developed are very easy to follow, and are without side effects. I would love to know what are your experiences regarding their usage. It would be wonderful to know and learn more about how more and more people delve deeper into their own personalities and discover the depth there in.

About the Author

Academician, consultant, and motivator Dr. Anupama Mudigonda shares her experiences over two decades, and discusses tools and techniques to fathom one's personality and shape one's image for enhanced fulfillment and success in the personal, professional and societal spheres and beyond. A PhD in marketing, from the University of Hyderabad, she works closely with people of all ages as a part of her mission 'U in the Universe' that aims to stir the basic consciousness for building a better tomorrow.

"Don't wait for someone to inspire you".

You can make a difference too, as its time to build a better YOU! So, get ready to put your best personality forward.

www.ingramcontent.com/pod-product-compliance
Lightning Source LLC
Chambersburg PA
CBHW072203170526
45158CB00004BB/1750